IN SOMERSET'S SKIES

IN SOMERSET'S SKIES

COLIN CRUDDAS

AMBERLEY

Front Cover: 'Crikey' was the appendage given by local inhabitants to the Westland Whirlwind when it first appeared in 1939.

Rear Cover: 'He's Behind You!' The Royal Navy Historic Flight's Swordfish makes a pass at an unsuspecting (?) Yeovilton Wren.

First published 2010

Amberley Publishing Plc
Cirencester Road, Chalford,
Stroud, Gloucestershire, GL6 8PE

www.amberley-books.com

Copyright © Colin Cruddas 2010

The right of Colin Cruddas to be identified as the Author
of this work has been asserted in accordance with the
Copyrights, Designs and Patents Act 1988.

British Library Cataloguing in Publication Data.
A catalogue record for this book is available from the British Library.

ISBN 978 1 4456 0024 6

Typeset in 10pt on 12pt Sabon.
Typesetting and Origination by Fonthill.
Printed in the UK.

Dedication

Fred Ballam, CEng, FRAeS.

To my knowledge, Fred Ballam, who sadly died during the compilation of this work, did not write a book of his own.

What he did do, however, was to provide invaluable assistance to many others, who, like myself, would have fallen at the first hurdle. Fred, who began his long aeronautical career at Westland in the 1940s, went on, in retirement, to become the company's archivist.

During this seventy-year working span, he gained an immense knowledge of aviation, which he freely shared and which will be sorely missed.

I therefore think it entirely appropriate to dedicate this modest offering to Westland's long-serving historian and my good friend, who, true to form, provided many of the illustrations for this book.

A busy scene at Bristol Airport, Lulsgate, 2010.

Contents

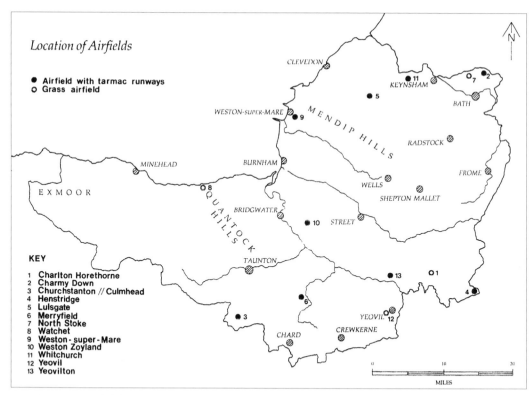

Location of Airfields

● Airfield with tarmac runways
○ Grass airfield

KEY

1 Charlton Horethorne
2 Charmy Down
3 Churchstanton // Culmhead
4 Henstridge
5 Lulsgate
6 Merryfield
7 North Stoke
8 Watchet
9 Weston-super-Mare
10 Weston Zoyland
11 Whitchurch
12 Yeovil
13 Yeovilton

Somerset Airfields	OS Reference
Charlton Hawthorne	ST643244
Charmy Down	ST764700
Culmhead/Church Stanton	ST208154
Henstridge	ST752205
Lulsgate Bottom	ST504651
Merryfield	ST342186
Weston-Super-Mare	ST345602
Weston Zoyland	ST365345
Whitchurch	ST595686
Yeovil	ST540158
Yeovilton	ST554234

Introduction

Yorkshire, Lincolnshire, Norfolk and Suffolk have, because of their wartime strategic locations, long been regarded as 'Bomber Country'. Similarly, the Home Counties, and those along the lower east and south coasts, are now traditionally regarded as the main hosts of the fighter squadrons whose epic deeds in 1940 saved Britain from invasion.

Other areas, less frequently involved with front-line activities, have, nevertheless, contributed greatly to Service and civil aviation's achievements and to the nation's aeronautical development. Somerset can rightly claim such recognition, having provided a significant number of air training and operational facilities for RAF and RN use, in some cases before, but mainly throughout and beyond, the Second World War. In addition to this, the original Westland Aircraft Works, after many changes having now become the UK element of AgustaWestland, itself wholly owned by the Italian giant Finmeccanica, continues to be a major European centre for rotary and fixed-wing aircraft development and manufacture.

AgustaWestland's manufacturing site at Yeovil, the RNAS establishment at Yeovilton, and Bristol Airport currently dominate Somerset's aviation scene. But other, now long-defunct Service bases, along with once-major civic aerodromes at Whitchurch and Weston-Super-Mare, have also played key roles in the county's aviation history. In recalling their contributions, mainly in pictures, I have relied heavily on the good offices and expert advice of Westland archivists Fred Ballam and Dave Gibbings and their colleague Mike Burrow, the admirable co-operation provided by director Graham Mottram's staff at Yeovilton's Fleet Air Arm Museum, and that of Bristol Airport's Community Relations Manager, Mike Littleton. However, I would be greatly remiss if I failed to offer my most grateful thanks to Duncan Greenman of the Bristol Airchive, Phil Jarrett, Mike Hooks and Nick Stroud of *Aeroplane*, Paul Jarvis and Jim Davies at the British Airways Museum, Air Britain's Dave Partington, Ian Harris of the Royal Air Force Weston Zoyland Research Group, and to fellow scribes Peter Amos, Peter Campbell, Mac Hawkins, Derek James, and Graham Smith, all of whom have dug deep into their memories and photographic collections.

Though having earlier produced similar volumes covering air activity in Dorset, Hampshire, and Wiltshire, my more recent literary efforts have been diverted into other channels. It was only after the prompting by an ex-RNVR pilot, Bernard Pike (National Service, would you believe – how lucky can you get?), I realised that yet another county, Somerset no less, might benefit from some further pictorial exposure. Intended to be a representative reflection rather than a definitive history, hopefully, this slender volume will serve to both please and inform.

Lastly, my grateful thanks go to Heather Trippick and my daughter Sally for gallantly retyping my manuscript following its mysterious departure from my computer , and to my wife, Thelma, for bringing my frequent grammatical excursions back on track.

Inevitably, in works of this kind, it is impossible to trace the true origins of all the material used. Although I have made great efforts to do so, I offer my advance apologies for any misplaced credits, errors, or omissions. Please don't shoot the messenger; I shall try and do better next time!

Colin Cruddas
Shaftesbury 2010

Chapter One

Go West, Young Man

So, where and when did aviation in Somerset begin? In 1915, and following a plea by the Munitions Minister, Lloyd George, for industry to support the war effort, the offer by Petters Ltd, then a leading heavy-oil-engine manufacturer in Yeovil, to undertake aircraft production might be considered a reasonable starting point. However, although this led to the immediate award of a contract to construct twelve Short 184 seaplanes, such a claim would be somewhat of a late-starter, for the county can boast a much earlier aerial connection.

The preceding century had seen much theoretical consideration given to achieving flight by heavier-than-air machines driven by mechanical methods. Such inventive 'advancements', though entirely commendable, were invariably thwarted by the lack of a lightweight propulsive system. Steam power had, in the meantime, become fashionable and used in applications where the weight of the body to be propelled was of little relative importance, i.e., on the land or at sea, it proved to be a revolutionary moving force. In matters of the air, however, where weight was already known to be a critical factor, the aeronautical adventurers of the day had little choice but to hope that, though heavy and cumbersome, steam-driven means of providing thrust would, nevertheless, help mankind to achieve parity with the birds.

Thus it came about that, in the early 1840s, a meeting of the minds took place when a Yorkshireman, W. S. Henson, who had already conceived what he grandly described as an Aerial Steam Carriage, linked forces with John Stringfellow, then a resident of Chard in Somerset, to produce a more practical working version. Unfortunately, the combined efforts of these far-sighted pioneers were to prove unsuccessful, although Stringfellow did, in 1848, by then again working alone, construct a steam-driven model that was officially accredited with being the first powered device to fly. But it was not until 1903, when the Wright brothers achieved not only powered but *controlled* ascents in their Flyer I, that the long-awaited breakthrough in manned flight occurred. Along with Sir George Cayley, F. S. Wenham, F. W. Lanchester, and other British engineers and designers, John Stringfellow was rightly considered to have made a significant contribution to aviation's progress. In recognition of this, an English Heritage plaque now marks the site, in Chard, where his early endeavours took place.

The twin Petter brothers, Percival Waddams (left) and Sir Ernest Willoughby, founded the Westland company in 1915.

The site of the first business acquired by the Petter twins' father, then called the Nautilus Works, is now Yeovil's First Group bus garage and located on the Reckleford dual carriageway at Goldcroft.

John Stringfellow (1799-1883), aviation pioneer.

Though born at Attercliffe in Yorkshire, Stringfellow, following the family lace-making business, later took up residence in Chard's High Street.

Stringfellow's 3-metre-span model was the first machine to fly using mechanical motive power (steam). It now resides in the Science Museum at Kensington.

Somerset's first aviation pioneer has a suitably honoured resting place in Chard's cemetery.

Somerset's introduction to aircraft manufacture. Short 184 seaplanes under construction at Yeovil.

'Home James and don't spare the horses' – Short seaplane wings en-route to Hamble, via Yeovil Junction in January 1916.

A Short 184 fully assembled at Hamble prepares to get its feet wet.

Another Westland-built product, this time a Short 166, showing its distinctive ailerons in 'drooped' position. A Short 184 sits behind.

Returning now to 1915, the Petter brothers' introduction to aircraft manufacture brought an instant need for larger premises. Fortunately, Petters had already acquired Westland Farm, located on the western outskirts of Yeovil, where it was intended to build a much needed forge to support their engine and fireplace business. The site proved ideal for the establishment of an aircraft works and, later, an airfield. Management changes were also introduced that included the recruitment of Commander Robert Bruce, RN, a former manager of the Bristol-based British & Colonial Aircraft Company, to head the new aircraft business, and the transfer, from Petters Ltd, of Arthur Davenport to become chief draughtsman. This general restructuring enabled the first Short 184 to be delivered on time, in January 1916. Having ably demonstrated its manufacturing capability, the company then received a subsequent order for twenty Short 166 seaplanes, but because a full set of engineering drawings was not forthcoming, a properly organised Drawing Office had to be set up to co-ordinate the technical effort with Shorts. The newly named Westland Aircraft Works, having rapidly gained experience and confidence, then embarked on the independent design and manufacture of two small N1B Scout seaplanes, which carried the serial numbers N.16 and N.17. These were followed, towards the end of the war, by two landplane fighters – the Wagtail and a two-seater version, the Weasel – but with general aircraft production at its wartime peak, orders were not received. Fortunately, continuous subcontracted work on Sopwith 1½ Strutters, DH.4s, DH.9s, DH.9As, and Vickers Vimy bombers allowed the Yeovil workforce to produce a grand total of 808 machines during the war years. In 1917, the construction of a new 140-foot-span Vimy erection hangar (the largest in the United Kingdom) and the acquiring of additional land for an airfield directly alongside the works placed Westland in a seemingly enviable position for independent postwar work. It was, however, only the extended production of the Vimy and especially that of the DH.9A, of which Westland eventually built 400, that kept the Yeovil factory in being and ready to embark on civil designs.

Westland's first attempt at an independent design was the N1B naval fighter powered by a 150-hp Bentley AR 1 rotary engine. Shown here is N 16, the first of two to be built at the end of the First World War.

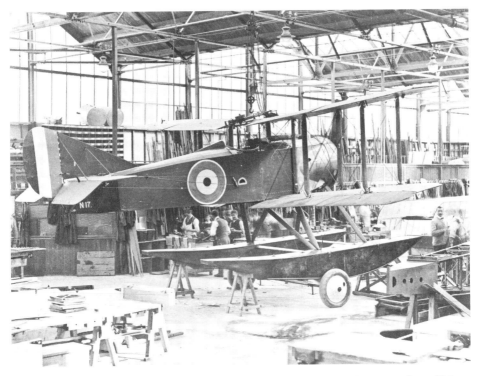

Westland's N 17, under assembly at Yeovil. Note the different float layout to that of N 16.

The Wagtail was Westland's first attempt at single-seat fighter design. Shown here is the third of the five machines built between 1917 and 1920.

More ambitious was the Weasel, essentially a two-seat scaled-up version of the Wagtail. Intended to replace the Bristol F.2B Fighter in postwar service, problems with the notoriously unreliable ABC Dragonfly engine led to late deliveries, which coincided with the general cancellation of military contracts. Four Weasels were built at Yeovil and all were passed on to the Royal Aircraft Establishment at Farnborough for test-flying and engine-development work.

A total of 125 Sopwith 1½ Strutters filled the Westland production lines in 1916/1917.

The finished product. A Sopwith 1½ Strutter awaits delivery from Yeovil.

The lack of workers in this picture, taken in dawn's early light, might imply a lack of urgency in Westland's war effort. This was, of course, entirely misleading, with DH.4s, DH.9s, DH.9As (shown here in 1918) accompanying Short and Sopwith machines off the production lines.

The DH.9 as originally equipped with the Puma engine.

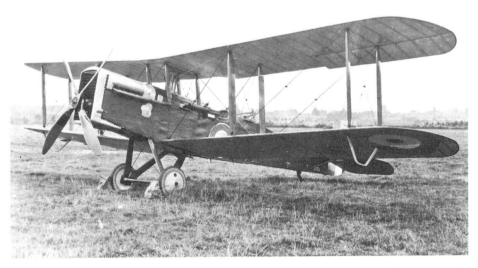

Westland redesigned the DH.9 to accommodate the American Liberty and Rolls-Royce Eagle engines and thus became the Design Authority on what was then designated the DH 9A.

A rare bird was this DH 9R, featuring an Armstrong Siddeley Jaguar engine, visiting Yeovil in the mid-1920s.

A contract for seventy-five Vickers Vimy bombers brought about the construction, in 1918, of a large-span hangar capable of housing six machines. However, contract cancellations resulted in only twenty-five being built.

Built during the First World War, the Westland wind-tunnel was one of the first to be installed by a manufacturer.

The Vickers Vimy, 'fore and aft', as produced by Westland. These were test-flown by Martlesham test pilot Sqn Ldr Rollo de Haga Haigh, who even managed to loop one!

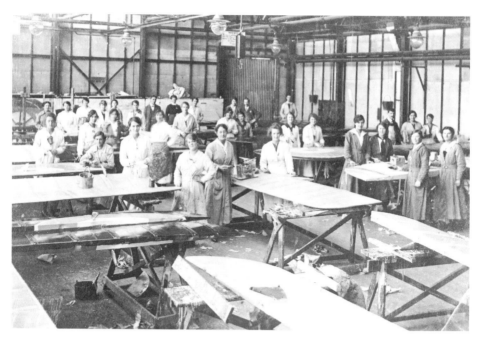

Westland's female workforce made an immense contribution to the company's wartime output. Shown here are the ladies of the Paint and Dope shop working on Vimy control surfaces in November 1918.

It must be conceded that the male labour force also had 'a hand in things', as witnessed by these chaps working hard to impress their work colleagues as the war ended.

Chapter Two

Gaining Strength

Following the Armistice in 1918, the Westland Company, along with every other aircraft manufacturer, faced great uncertainty and an ever-present threat of closure. Despite its hard-won wartime reputation, the Petter brothers now saw the Aircraft Works mainly as a useful, if probably short-term, cash contributor to the core business of oil-engine production. In attempting to diversify, piano manufacture was undertaken, which, given the presence of a foundry capable of making the frames and a workforce experienced in woodworking, was a logical attempt to utilise in-house skills. However, problems with the trade unions soon caused this approach to be abandoned and a safer path was pursued in light engineering and the production of milk churns!

The end of the war saw the RAF greatly over-resourced with 22,500 aircraft, 700 airfields and 290,000 personnel. Unsurprisingly, many existing aircraft were soon scrapped and production contracts cancelled, but a number of Vimy bombers were converted for peacetime use. It was this aeroplane that, used for record-breaking first flights across the Atlantic, to Australia, and to South Africa, alongside similarly converted machines from the de Havilland and Handley Page factories, helped to usher in British civil airline operations in the immediate postwar period.

Down in Yeovil, serious thought was also being given to passenger-carrying aircraft, and in late 1918, Arthur Davenport began initial design work on the Westland Limousine. No doubt influenced by the firm's association with the DH.9A, the four- and later six-seater Limousine bore a striking resemblance to this well-proven machine, and in 1920, it even won an Air Ministry competition for transport aircraft. However, the expected boom in postwar commercial flying failed to materialise, and only a small number later saw service in both Britain and Newfoundland. Drawing on its DH.9A experience even further, the company went on to produce the Westland Walrus. In fairness, it must be said that this aircraft, ungainly in both handling and appearance, was originally conceived elsewhere (at Armstrong Whitworth Ltd), and was only later handed over to Westland for design refinement and production. Despite its aesthetic shortcomings, thirty-six were built and served with reasonable distinction in the mid-1920s as carrier-borne fleet spotters with the Royal Navy.

Westland's first official test pilot was Captain Stuart Keep, who, after working with the Air Ministry in a similar capacity, joined the company in December 1918. Having successfully coped with the flight-testing of the Limousine and the Walrus, Keep then found himself faced with taking the firm's new Dreadnought airliner into the air.

The Petter brothers, their wives, and company officials, accompany the Director of Civil Aviation, Sir Sefton Brancker (second from right), during his visit to Yeovil following the Armistice.

Westland's first venture into commercial aircraft design was the Limousine, though only a small number entered service.

Limousines I (left) and II were fitted with Rolls-Royce Falcon and American Liberty engines.

The six-seat Limousine was a much larger variant, fitted with the more powerful 450-hp Napier Lion engine.

Though not a pretty sight and said by test pilot Captain Keep to possess vicious characteristics, the Westland Walrus was accepted for naval reconnaissance duties in the early 1920s. Unsuprisingly, the original production order was not increased.

Though great hopes were placed in the Dreadnought Postal Monoplane, it failed to survive its first flight, test pilot Stuart Keep being fortunate to have escaped with his life, though not his limbs, still intact.

To even consider a monoplane design was advanced thinking in the early 1920s. The company's belief in Woyevodsky's proposal was, despite the unfortunate outcome, courageous and entirely in keeping with the adventurous spirit of the age.

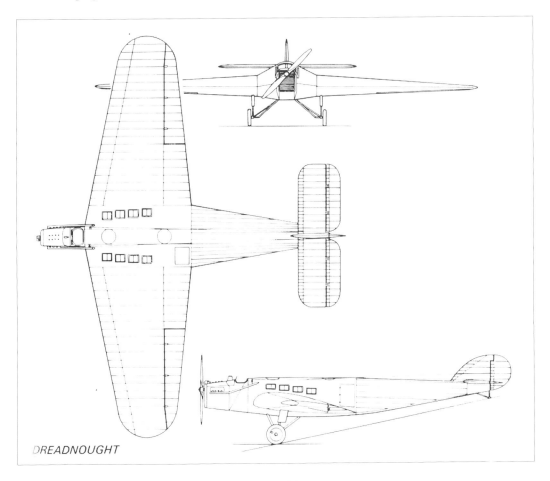

DREADNOUGHT

The first and second Westland Woodpigeons G-EBIY and G-EBJV, the latter now fitted with an ABC Scorpion II Engine, pictured at Yeovil in the early 1920s.

This was a futuristic 'blended wing/fuselage' design, based on a proposal put forward by a Russian engineer, M. Woyevodsky. Embodying a thick wing section intended to house passengers inboard of the engines, it was certainly an adventurous concept and way ahead of the ex-wartime biplane conversions of the day. Unfortunately, the Dreadnought proved to be a step too far, for after having completed high-speed taxiing tests that included one or two unintentional hops into the air, it barely got off the ground on its first real flight before it stalled and crashed. Captain Keep, though sustaining injuries that ended his test-flying career, did, nevertheless, continue to serve the company well in a technical and managerial capacity, until his retirement in 1935.

In 1924, the Air Ministry, realising that a new approach had to be made to interest the public in aviation, held a competition for light aircraft at Lympne in Kent. Westland, undecided as to whether to enter a biplane or monoplane, played safe and entered one of each type. The Woodpigeon was a biplane of conventional design, whilst the Widgeon was a high-wing monoplane featuring decidedly more racy lines. In the event, neither distinguished itself, largely because of inadequate engine power and the high purchasing cost. Later tests proved the Widgeon to be technically superior, but little headway was made, due largely to the official reluctance, then prevailing, to encourage monoplanes for Service use.

By the mid-1920s, the RAF's requirement for a DH.9A replacement saw Westland produce the Yeovil bomber, but this too failed to win favour, a rival machine, the Hawker Horsley, winning the coveted production order. Undeterred, the company then placed its faith in the Westbury, a twin-engined, three-seat biplane fighter that incorporated an unusual armament arrangement. This consisted of two 37-mm automatic shell-firing

The first Woodpigeon was entered No. 5 in the Lympne Light Aircraft Trials of 1924. Ease of manhandling is clearly demonstrated here.

The high-wing monoplane Widgeon I was Westland's alternative contender in the Lympne trials.

One very careless apprentice, 'experimenting' with matches and petrol, caused a fire that destroyed this Bessoneaux hangar at Yeovil in May 1918. The prototype Wagtail was badly damaged and a Sopwith Pup lost in the blaze.

Westland's Yeovil light bomber failed to impress the Air Ministry. Three examples were built during 1924-25, which, after Service evaluation, were used for research. Shown here is J7510, sporting prominent over-wing fuel tanks.

guns, one mounted in a rotatable nose turret, the other being arranged to fire forward over the centre section at an elevated angle. Though unusual in interwar fighter designs, this layout and the one later incorporated in the Westland COW (Coventry Ordnance Works) Gun Fighter were forerunners of the upward-firing cannon concept (*Schräge Musik*) used to such devastating effect by German night-fighters during the Second World War.

Although Westland failed to win contracts for the Yeovil, its new Westbury or Wizard monoplane fighters, or even the Witch, then being proposed as a replacement for the Horsley, the company finally achieved a sales breakthrough with the Widgeon III. This was an attractive parasol-winged light aeroplane that was frequently and skilfully demonstrated by the company's test pilots Laurence Openshaw and Harald Penrose. Sadly, both Openshaw, flying a Widgeon, and Sqn Leader Walter Longton, piloting a Blackburn Bluebird, were killed when their aircraft collided at the Bournemouth Whitsun Air Meeting on 4 June 1927.

Westland, though a founder member of the Society of British Aircraft Manufacturers, was by the mid-1920s still struggling to gain stature alongside its more established West Country rivals, the Bristol Aeroplane Co. Ltd, and the Gloster Aircraft Co. Ltd. Significant progress was made, however, with the design and development of the Wapiti

The Westland Westbury was a fighter/bomber escort design that featured an unusual armament layout then in favour with several leading French companies. This saw an upward-firing heavy-calibre gun mounted in the nose and mid-ship cockpits. Two Westbury prototypes were built, but by the time trials were completed, official interest in heavily armed multi-crew fighters had waned.

General Purpose machine. The need for such an aircraft had become increasingly evident when the policing duties placed upon the RAF in the Middle East, Afghanistan, and India's north-west frontier called for a machine with an all-round performance and load-carrying capability superior to that of the DH.9A. Having absorbed the lessons from the ill-fated Yeovil bomber exercise, the company then produced in the Wapiti, an economic proposal that took full advantage of the DH.9A's best design features and which astutely allowed stocks of existing spares to be used up. In so doing, it successfully fought off severe competition from Armstrong Whitworth, Bristol, de Havilland, Fairey, Gloster, and Vickers – no mean achievement in an era when each contract was a 'red in tooth and claw' battle for survival! Some eleven RAF squadrons were eventually equipped with Wapitis for foreign duties, and a further nine squadrons were employed into the mid-1930s in the day-bomber role with the Auxiliary Air Force. In total, well over 1,000 Wapitis and its final development, the Wallace, were built, allowing, at that time, the type to see more service in various parts of the world than any other aircraft serving with the Commonwealth air forces.

Wizard striptease! This pleasing monoplane, which appeared in the mid-1920s, represented a significant change in Westland's approach to fighter design. Dressed or undressed, the Wizard failed to unlock the stony coffers of the Air Ministry, whose preference for biplanes remained firmly entrenched.

Not entirely dissimilar in outward appearance to the Wizard, the Witch was a monoplane submission to a 1925 Air Ministry requirement for a two-seat, single-engined high-altitude day bomber to replace the Hawker Horsley. Following what now, in hindsight, was an inevitable path where official requirements were concerned, Westland's submission, along with those of its competitors, failed to get a tick in the acceptance column.

The Widgeon III and IIIA proved to be one of the turning points in Westland's fortunes. Though proving very popular in civil flying circles, the Widgeon found its production having to take second place to that of the military Wapiti.

This picture shows Westland Wapiti IIAs on the production line at Yeovil in 1928.

A Wapiti IIA ready for army co-operation duties with No. 27 Sqn in India in 1933.

Wapitis of No. 600 Sqn in 1935.

A Westland Wallace II before delivery from Yeovil to an operational unit. The Wallace was the first aircraft to enter RAF service that featured an enclosed cockpit.

Chapter Three

Flying Through the Thirties

No mention of Westland in the interwar period would be complete without reference to Captain Geoffrey Hill and his unique Pterodactyl (winged finger) flying-wing concept. Hill's design philosophy was, indeed, visionary, for not dissimilar configurations were produced in pre-war Germany by Lippisch and Horten, and later, by Handley Page (Manx), de Havilland (DH 108), Armstrong Whitworth (AW 52), and Shorts (Sherpa) when undertaking British postwar research into tailless aircraft.

Hill's association with Westland began in 1926, and it was in that year that the British public saw this revolutionary machine for the first time, when the Pterodactyl I led the fly-past of new types at the RAF's Hendon Display. Cautious development of such a radical design was clearly necessary and major consideration was given to eventually producing a highly manoeuvrable fighter, but by the time the final version, the Pterodactyl V, had completed its experimental flying in late 1935, it was belatedly judged to have little military or commercial potential. With Westland then reverting to more conventional designs, Captain Hill moved on to become Professor of Engineering at London University and, later, consulting engineer to both Shorts and General Aircraft. It may be added here that, in 1944, at the time when the Brabazon Committee's recommendations for Britain's postwar civil transport designs were being considered, Shorts, working closely with Captain Hill, proposed a large-scale Pterodactyl VIII transatlantic airliner, powered by five Rolls-Royce Griffon engines. Armstrong Whitworth was another company attracted to the advanced flying-wing airliner concept, but again, more conservative approaches were to win the day.

Westland's Interceptor fighter was another attempt by Arthur Davenport to introduce a monoplane configuration into Service use. Designed to meet Air Ministry Specification F.20/27, and powered by, firstly, a Bristol Mercury and, later, a Jupiter engine, it included several advanced features, such as using the engine exhaust gas for gun heating and the provision of both an oxygen system and W/T equipment. Unfortunately, the Interceptor lacked the performance of other competitors and the sole example was later seconded to the Royal Aircraft Establishment at Farnborough for engine development work. A follow-up design, the COW Gun Fighter (already referred to), first flew in 1931, but it too achieved little success when changes in the RAF's fighting tactics caused the specification to be cancelled.

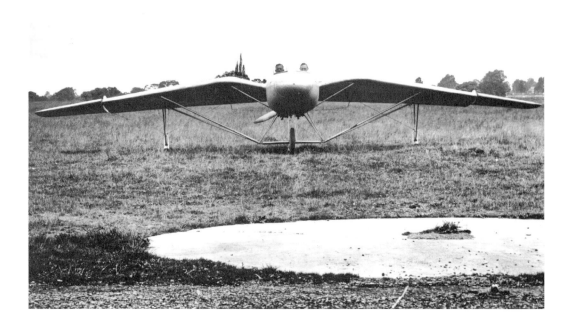

These pages: Captain Hill's Pterodactyl 1 concept appeared in various forms between its first appearance in 1926 and its final abandonment in 1937. Shown here are the 1A and 1B variants. The 'undressed' picture clearly shows the Pterodactyl 1A's torque tube arrangement for operating wing-tip control surfaces.

These pages: Though clearly following the 'winged finger' layout of the earlier Mk 1 variants, the Pterodactyl Mk IV featured a three-seat enclosed cabin and a more powerful 120-hp Gipsy III engine. It also included a rudimentary variable-wing sweepback system that allowed some five degrees of movement. Though dramatically painted to represent its fearsome forebear at the 1932 RAF Display at Hendon, it was not considered likely to make a mark on either the civil or military markets and did not enter production.

Despite giving a firm impression of a modern day, albeit heavily overpowered, microlight, the Pterodactyl Mk V was designed as a turret fighter. First taking to the air in 1934, it was reported to be an intrinsically sound design, but a shortage of Goshawk engines created a problem when the one fitted to the prototype was seriously damaged following seizure on take-off. Hopes for the Pterodactyl as a viable concept were finally over.

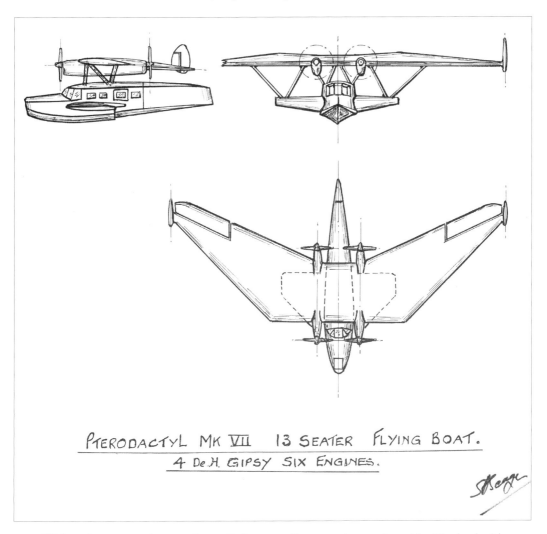

PTERODACTYL MK VII 13 SEATER FLYING BOAT.

4 De.H. GIPSY SIX ENGINES.

Well, perhaps not quite over, for preliminary studies were also conducted by Westland with Saunders-Roe regarding the building of a thirteen-seat flying-boat navigational trainer based on the Pterodactyl wing platform. However, Captain Hill's departure from the firm soon saw enthusiasm for the project evaporate.

These pages: Determined to follow the constantly changing trail of Air Ministry fighter specifications, Westland produced, in the late 1920s, firstly, the Interceptor (top left), armed with two Vickers .303 machine guns and the COW Gun Fighter, shown here, dressed and undressed, displaying its 37-mm heavy artillery.

Still striving to enter the fighter arena, Westland then produced the F.7/30, which, by Air Ministry decree, was required to incorporate the new evaporatively cooled Goshawk engine. Though great hopes were placed on this method of cooling, the problems experienced at Rolls-Royce resulted in a greatly extended development period. This led not only to the Goshawk's abandonment but also to that of Westland's airframe contender and several other proposed designs all hoping to win a large production order.

Though facing continual discouragement on the military side, Westland introduced a series of biplane prototypes as private ventures. The first of these, the PV.3, built in 1931, along with the prototype Wallace (originally known as the PV.6), demonstrated good high-altitude capabilities and gained immense publicity for the firm when forming part of the Houston Mount Everest Expedition in 1933. It was also in this year and the early part of 1934 that Westland, taking on whatever work it could, built the sole Hendy Heck. This was a two-seat cabin monoplane designed for the personal use of Whitney Straight, head of the Straight Corporation that was soon to take over the airport at Weston-Super-Mare.

Opposite and above: Westland's F.7/30 was designed to the same demanding specification as the successful Gloster Gladiator but was unfortunate in having to incorporate the infamous Goshawk engine. Both ground shots were taken before first flight. Also shown is an extremely rare picture of K2891 in flight.

Westland's private venture PV.3 gained fame when, in 1933, as G-ACAZ and renamed the Houston-Westland PV.3, it shared with the modified Westland PV.6/Wallace prototype, G-ACBR, shown here, the distinction of being the first machine to fly over Mount Everest – a feat then seen as tantamount to landing on the moon!

Orders of any kind were more than welcome in Westland during the Depression years, including one to build this Hendy Heck for Whitney Straight in 1934.

Westland re-entered the civil transport field with the Mk IV, six-seat tri-motor, designed for domestic routes. Shown here is G-AAGW, which served in Imperial Airway's private hire section for charter flights.

This Westland Wessex, powered by three Genet Major engines was one of four supplied to Belgium's SABENA Airways.

Edward, Prince of Wales, inspects G-ABVB, scheduled for delivery to the Portsmouth, Southsea, & Isle of Wight Aviation Company in 1931.

Westland's PV.7, both stripped to the bare essentials and, equipped with a dummy torpedo, dressed for action. Designed as a two-seater to meet Air Ministry General Specification G.4/31, it was not proceeded with, following the crash of the sole prototype, from which Harald Penrose escaped by parachute.

It was almost ten years after its first foray with the Limousine before the company made another venture into multi-passenger aircraft manufacture. This resulted in a six-seat, high-wing, tri-motor monoplane (no doubt a monoplane at Davenport's insistence) designated the Westland IV. The prototype was actually constructed and flown in 1929, but it was its immediate production derivative, the Wessex, ten of which were built, that saw useful service throughout the 1930s with, mainly, the Belgian airline SABENA, the Portsmouth, Southsea & Isle of Wight Aviation Company, and Sir Alan Cobham's touring air displays.

Continuing the private venture series, the PV.7 was aimed at providing the RAF with a successor to the Wapiti and the Wallace. However, whilst undergoing official trials at Martlesham Heath in August 1934, a main support strut failure caused the complete collapse of the entire wing structure and test pilot Harald Penrose to make one of the first parachute departures from an enclosed-cockpit military aeroplane. Despite the aircraft's undoubted potential, the cost of producing a second privately funded prototype was considered to be too great, but Westland, persevering with its high-wing, single-engine monoplane series, was about to make an indelible mark on British aviation. This came about with the PV.8 Lysander, destined to become one of the most famous and instantly recognisable aircraft of the Second World War. Here, the reader may ponder on the choice of 'Lysander', which deviated from the usual company practice of choosing names beginning with 'W', even up to its final fixed-wing

Enter the Lysander. The first of 1,427 to be built at Westland's Yeovil and Doncaster factories between 1935 and 1942, K6127 took to the skies for the first time at Boscombe Down on 15 June 1936.

design, the Wyvern. The answer lies in the fact that with Westland having, in 1937, produced 178 Hawker Hectors under subcontract, it seemed a natural continuation to call its army co-operation work successor, 'Lysander', both being the names of ancient warrior heroes then linked together in a popular patriotic song of the time, 'The British Grenadiers':

Some speak of Alexander
And some of Hercules
Of Hector and Lysander
And such great names as these ...

At which point, the author's recollection of such stirring verses, sung in the wartime school hall with such pride, now seems a little dated!

On 4 July 1935, the Westland Aircraft Works ceased functioning as a branch of Petters Ltd to become Westland Aircraft Ltd, though the new organisation was still highly influenced at board level by the presence of Sir Ernest Petter as Chairman and Joint Managing Director. But in the mid-1930s, alongside its fixed-wing projects, Westland's designers were also collaborating with the Cierva Autogiro Company and a French firm, Avions Weymann-Lepere, with a view to building a new rotary-wing autogiro. Following on from the association with Captain Hill, this was yet another departure from the conventional design path, and although two prototypes, the C.29 and the CL.20, were constructed, the former failed to get off the ground and only some eight hours of useful test-flying were gained on the later machine. Though hardly an auspicious start, this early flirtation with rotary-wing design might now be regarded as a portent of things to come that would, eventually, greatly change the nature of the company.

As the 1930s progressed, further board and ownership changes took place at Westland when, firstly, John Brown Ltd acquired a controlling interest, this soon being followed by the entry of the Associated Electrical Industries Group. It was during this turbulent period of change that Sir Ernest Petter's son, Edward (Teddy), gained a quick promotion to Technical Director. His elevation was not viewed with great favour by certain other board members, and his forceful views soon led to the resignation of Robert Bruce. The dismissal of Stuart Keep, who, it will be recalled, was crippled for life in the Dreadnought crash, also to make way for Teddy Petter, was another unfortunate event that did not reflect well on the firm's executive management policy of the day.

In the mid-1930s, the increasing inevitability of war with Germany brought the country's defence needs under constant review. New Air Ministry specifications brought forth the Hurricane (1935) and the Spitfire (1936) high-speed, single-seat fighter prototypes, both production designs being later armed with eight machine guns. However, a further specification soon followed for a fighter equipped with six or eight 20-mm cannons. This, in turn, was changed to call for 20-mm or 23-mm cannons in 'sufficient numbers to meet a two-second-burst destructive effect'. Five companies responded, including Westland, which put forward a long-range twin-engined proposal, the PV.9, armed with four 20-mm cannons. The first prototype was completed in late September 1938, and flight trials continued through the following summer. Problems with the Rolls-Royce Peregrine engines, on top of those that invariably attend a new airframe, brought unwelcome delays, but a production order for 200 machines was eventually placed, though this was later reduced by half, for what had now become called the Whirlwind. Faced with this challenging work alongside large orders for the Lysander, Westland, in late 1939, now found itself firmly at war!

A cold, bleak Yeovil during the winter of 1939/40, with Lysanders awaiting delivery to Service units.

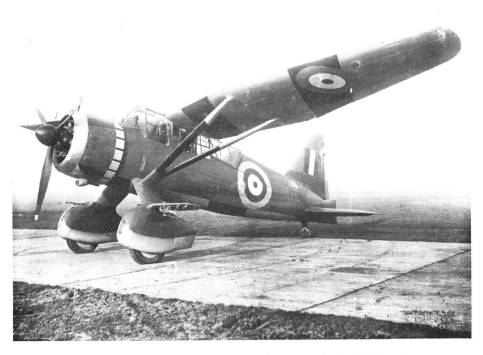

V 9905 was one of the last production models to leave Yeovil. The black and yellow underwing stripes indicate its target-towing role.

Though undoubtedly best remembered for its part in delivering Special Operations Executive agents to occupied Europe, the Lysander was considered for other unusual duties. The prototype, shown here reconfigured to include a tandem wing and a mock-up four-gun rear turret, investigated the type's potential as an anti-invasion 'beach strafer'; however, this odd-looking variant, designated the Westland P 12 Wendover, did not enter production.

The Hawker Hector's Napier Dagger engine installation with and without its well-tailored cowling.

Westland's collaboration with the Spanish autogiro designer Cierva produced the C.29. Built in 1933, it experienced severe vibration problems at one third of the rotor's take-off rpm and never got off the ground.

Having co-opted the assistance of French aeronautical engineer Georges Lepere, who had previously worked on Cierva's machines, Westland came up with the Pobjoy-powered CL.20. Though an improvement on the C.29, an inability to climb above 300 feet meant that, after just eight and a half hours of test-flying, the project was quietly put to rest in favour of more productive work.

William Edward Willoughby Petter. Though at times considered difficult to work with, he was, nevertheless, a highly gifted and innovative designer, largely responsible for the Lysander, Whirlwind and Welkin projects at Westland. In 1944, he joined the English Electric Company's Aviation Division and, as Chief Engineer, contributed greatly to the success of the Canberra before moving on to Folland Aircraft Ltd, where he became responsible for the Gnat lightweight fighter. He finally retired to Switzerland, where he died aged fifty-eight, in 1968.

Arthur Davenport, Harald Penrose and Robert Bruce at Yeovil in January in 1933.

The first prototype Whirlwind L6844 in dark-grey finish and black/white wing undersurfaces made its flight on 11 October 1938.

Although flight-testing of both Whirlwind prototypes L6844 and L6845 proceeded throughout 1939, problems with engine overheating gave continuous cause for concern.

The Westland factory and airfield in 1939.

DH. Dragon, G-ACMJ belonging to Norman Edgars, Western Airways at Weston-Super-Mare in 1938.

Chapter Four

On the Civil Side

In the interwar period, the de Havilland Moth, Blackburn Bluebird, Avro Avian, and the Westland Widgeon were the light aircraft types most popular with flying clubs, associations and private owners. However, the arrival of touring air displays, best exemplified by, firstly, in the early 1920s, the Berkshire Aviation Company and, later, Sir Alan Cobham's National Aviation Day Display, also brought a wide variety of other aircraft and aerial entertainment to towns and cities throughout the country. Bath, Wells, Frome, Weston-Super-Mare, Radstock, Taunton, and Glastonbury were popular county venues for shows provided by Cobham, Charles Barnard, CWA Scott, and other famous aviation luminaries in the 1930s. However, the most notable civil flying centre in Somerset at the time was the airport at Whitchurch, opened in May 1930 by Prince George, the Duke of Kent. Located in the northern sector of the county, it became home to the Bristol and Wessex Aeroplane Club, which first began operations at Filton aerodrome in 1927. Large crowds attended the airport, when, after becoming the third municipal aerodrome in the country, it provided an official check-point during the King's Cup Air Race in July 1930 and was subsequently the venue for other prestigious events, such as the RAF Pageants, in the years leading up to the Second World War. Whitchurch also played a key role in establishing a permanent air link between the South West and Ireland, for it saw the arrival of the first Aer Lingus flight, a D.H.84 Dragon, after the Irish airline's formation in 1936. By 1940, records show that the airport was processing some 4,000 passengers a year!

A major pre-war presence at Whitchurch was that of Airwork Ltd, which provided an aircraft maintenance and sales service. Also prominent was Norman Edgar, a successful local businessman whose budding airline and charter operations quickly mopped up any local competition, such as the two-passenger Desoutter operated by Bristol Air Taxis. By 1934, Edgar's Western Airways was operating between Bristol and Cardiff on an hourly basis, with four Dragons, two DH Rapides and two DH Puss Moths. It then proved but a short step to providing services linking towns on the South Coast with the Channel Islands, but a strong competitor soon appeared in the form of Railway Air Services (RAS), a newly constituted subsidiary of Imperial Airways. Also operating a fleet of Dragons and Dragon Rapides, RAS, with its greater financial backing and superior management, soon became the principle British domestic airline.

In 1939, the outbreak of war saw the Imperial Airways and British Airways fleets of land-based airliners congregate at Whitchurch to await their changeover to military duties and transfer to what would, on 1 April 1940, become the British Overseas Airways Corporation. For aviation enthusiasts, the sight of Armstrong Whitworth Ensigns, de Havilland Albatrosses, Lockheed 12s, Handley Page 42s, and the occasional Junkers 52 gathered en masse must, indeed, have been a sight to quicken the pulse. Many of these machines, in particular the HP 42s, were soon operating under the aegis of a new Air Ministry department, National Air Communications, to provide a trooping and cargo service for the British Expeditionary Force in France. This, however, proved to be a short-lived arrangement, for after the fall of France, the NAC was disbanded when such transportation was no longer required.

Formed in September 1939, the Air Transport Auxiliary was an organisation whose primary task was to release RAF aircrew from having to fly new machines from the factories to Service units. Initially consisting entirely of men, but later of both men and women pilots, its headquarters were located at White Waltham in Berkshire, but local pools of pilots and aircraft were soon set up around the country to service the more outlying factories. This arrangement saw three Avro Ansons and twelve pilots initially allocated to Whitchurch as B Section of No. 3 Ferry Pilots' Pool for the delivery of aircraft produced not only by the Bristol Aeroplane Company at Filton, but also those by Westland at Yeovil, Airspeed at Portsmouth and Christchurch, Supermarine and Cunliffe-Owen at Eastleigh, and also Portsmouth Aviation at Portsmouth. Following a general reorganisation, this was later designated No. 2 FPP. The bravery and determination of the ATA pilots is quite beyond an adequate description in this book, but fortunately, their unique efforts are well recorded elsewhere (see Recommended Reading).

Work on a new airport at Weston-Super-Mare began in February 1936 with the first services by Western Airways to Cardiff taking place in May. It was, perhaps, inevitable that some rivalry would arise between Whitchurch and what was seen as a new upstart operation just 'down the road', but with Norman Edgar having largely transferred his interests to Weston and the arrival of Crilly Airways to provide additional West Country services, Somerset's new facility was, it seemed, off to a flying start. Later, in 1939, a contract was placed with the Straight Corporation, then managing the aerodrome, to operate an Elementary and Reserve Flying Training School, but this was soon overtaken after war was declared by a requirement to provide navigational training, with Avro Ansons then taking over from the Tiger Moths.

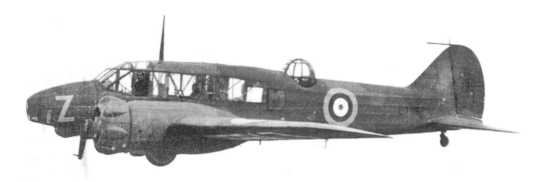

The Avro Anson was the Air Transport Auxiliary's choice of machine for transporting its pilots to and from the Ferry Pool bases such as Whitchurch.

Sir Alan Cobham was Britain's premier aviation showman in the interwar period. His National Aviation Day Display visited nearly a thousand locations in the British Isles during 1932-35·

On **THURSDAY, AUGUST 31st**

Between 3.0 and 3.30 p.m.

A HEIGHT JUDGING COMPETITION

for Readers of the

"Somerset County Gazette"

in conjunction with

SIR ALAN COBHAM'S

AIR DISPLAY

AT

Park Farm, West Buckland,

TAUNTON—WELLINGTON ROAD,

On **SUNDAY, SEPTEMBER 3rd.**

20 FREE FLIGHTS

AS PRIZES FOR OUR READERS.

In conjunction with Sir Alan Cobham the "Somerset County Gazette" has arranged that its readers shall have the opportunity of securing FREE FLIGHTS in one of the Air Liners which will be taking part in his display on September 3rd.

On THURSDAY, AUGUST 31st, between 3.0 and 3.30 p.m., a High Speed Single-seat Fighter of a type until recently used by the crack Fighter Squadrons of the Royal Air Force will fly over Taunton.

This 'plane will be readily recognised by its brilliant silver colouring and the roar of its 550 h.p. geared and super-charged Siddeley engine.

A THICK SCREEN OF BLOOD RED SMOKE

Will be released by the Machine during its Flight over Taunton.

Our readers are invited to estimate the height at which the aeroplane is flying when the smoke is emitted.

Tickets will be awarded to those who estimate the height correctly, or to those nearest. These Tickets will entitle the holders to Free Admission to the Display and a Twenty-five mile Cruise in an Airspeed Liner on SUNDAY, SEPTEMBER 3rd. Estimates of the height must be sent in on a Coupon cut from this issue (see below).

Cobham's displays were always highly organised affairs guaranteed to provide a feast of aerial entertainment. Many thrill-seekers had their first flight at events such as this held at West Buckland on 3 September 1933.

The Handley Page W.10 airliner and the Cierva C.19 were just two of the large and varied selection of machines provided by Cobham for passenger flights.

This page and next: The flying club facilities and clubhouse at Whitchurch exude a peacetime tranquillity in the early 1930s.

The Whitchurch clubhouse.

The popularity of pre-war aerial events may be gauged from this crowd at Whitchurch in 1931.

A close finish in the Whitchurch 1931 Aerial Summer Meet 'Utility Race' between crews of a Parnall Elf and a DH Puss Moth.

RAS routes included Whitchurch in the mid-1930s.

The Handley Page 42 was, by 1940, totally obsolete and overtaken by more modern designs. However, it proved it still had a part to play in wartime operations, supplying materials to British troops in France.

'Ensign' and 'Everest' look purposeful in wartime camouflage at Whitchurch. Both aircraft were powered by 950-hp Wright Cyclone engines.

Airliners en masse! Lockheed 12s dominate the foreground, whilst the bigger boys, a Junkers 52, a DH Albatross, and two Ensigns, sit behind awaiting new wartime duties.

KLM DC.3 'Ibis', in which actor Leslie Howard lost his life, was a frequent visitor to Whitchurch.

The ubiquitous Tiger Moth equipped the RAF's Elementary and Reserve Flying Training School at Weston-Super-Mare in 1939.

The Anson displaced the Tiger Moth when Weston became a navigational training base.

Chapter Five

Industry's Call to Arms

In September 1939, Westland found itself under the firm hand of Managing Director Eric Mensforth. The firm's premises at Yeovil and Ilchester were quickly and effectively camouflaged and directed toward the production and repair of existing types rather than new aircraft development. This effort, which extended until 1946, was not unlike that of the company in the First World War and largely involved the subcontracted manufacture of other firms' designs, which included the Barracuda, the Spitfire, and also the Seafire, for which Westland retained design authority until the type was finally withdrawn from service.

Alongside this, the Bristol Aeroplane Company operated shadow factories at Old Mixon and at Banwell, both sites located near Weston-Super-Mare, which concentrated mainly on the assembly of the Bristol Beaufighter. At peak production, ninety aircraft were being turned out each month and by the end of the war, a grand total of 3,336 Beaufighters had been delivered from these sites. From 1943, the Banwell factory also constructed Beaufort torpedo bombers and, later, thirty-six Hawker Tempest II fighters destined for operations in the Far East, the first flight of a Banwell-built Tempest taking place on 4 October 1944.

The Westland Company did not, however, experience lasting success with either of its own twin-engined fighter designs, the Whirlwind or the Welkin. Though highly innovative, Teddy Petter's technical leadership proved to be unsettling, major disagreements frequently occurring with Arthur Davenport's design team and test pilot Harald Penrose over structural and system configurations. Not least of these occurred following Petter's unorthodox decision to route the Whirlwind's engine exhaust pipes through ducts in the wing fuel tanks. Despite the safety concerns expressed by senior design staff, Petter's insistence on this potentially dangerous arrangement nearly brought about a catastrophic failure when, during a test flight, part of the exhaust ducting burnt through. Luckily, this occurred in an engine nacelle and not a tank, but it still brought about a malfunction of the aileron control system and major control problems. Penrose later commented that he had 'a worrying half-hour' whilst he cautiously skidded the aircraft back to Boscombe Down using rudder and mismatched engine power to 'get round the corners'.

Still on a whimsical note, Penrose also recalled his shocked surprise whilst test-flying an unarmed Whirlwind, to suddenly find himself in the company of a German fighter. Both he and his likely adversary then sought immediate sanctuary in nearby cloud, leaving Penrose to believe that the sight of four, albeit empty cannons, aggressively protruding from his aircraft's nose had left the enemy more unnerved than himself!

'Teddy' Petter, Eric Mensforth and Air Marshal Sir Wilfred Freeman accompany HM King George VI during a visit to Yeovil in 1941.

Westland's Drawing Office was typical of those throughout the aircraft industry until computers took over from drawing boards in the 1980s.

Wartime at Westland. Seafire and Welkin fighters share a Yeovil production assembly shop in February 1944.

A subcontracted Fairey Barracuda awaits flight test at Westland's airfield. Note the barrage balloon used for airfield defence in the background.

Spitfire Vbs under repair at Westland's Contractor Repair Organisation base at Ilchester.

Spitfire VIIIs in North African camouflage sit alongside Lysanders at Ilchester.

A total of 5,564 Bristol Beaufighters were built in Great Britain (and 362 in Australia), of which some two thirds were built and test-flown from the Bristol shadow factory at Old Mixon near Weston-Super-Mare.

The Bristol Aeroplane Company also operated a shadow factory at Banwell producing Beaufort torpedo bombers and, later, a small number of Tempest II fighters.

The requirement for a non-traversable weapon arrangement dictated a twin-engined configuration for the Whirlwind. The end result, most pleasing to the eye, is well demonstrated as Penrose breaks to starboard.

Harald Penrose flying an unarmed Whirlwind. Here, the clean lines of the engine cowling can be seen to good effect.

The Whirlwind's cockpit of 1941. Missing from the right-hand side is the IFF recognition indicator.

Once seen, or heard, never forgotten! Though the Whirlwind experienced only limited operational success, it was an impressive machine that incorporated many innovative design features.

Shown in peacetime livery, this Whirlwind served as a company hack between 1945-47.

October 1942 and an unwelcoming wet day at Yeovil sees the prototype Welkin about to undergo engine runs before its first flight.

The Whirlwind, though possessing many advanced aerodynamic, structural and system features, became a victim of contract reduction when the original Ministry order for 200 machines was lowered to 114. Not for the first time (shades of the F.7/30's dependence on the Goshawk powerplant ten years earlier), a promising Westland design found itself consigned to the sidelines when the Ministry of Aircraft Production and Rolls-Royce agreed to terminate production of the Peregrine engine. Releasing the company to concentrate its output on the Merlin can, in the light of events, hardly be criticised, for the de Havilland Mosquito, a clear beneficiary of this policy, proved well able to undertake the fighter and ground attack roles originally envisaged for the Whirlwind.

The prototype Welkin, which first flew in November 1942, was a direct result of a 1938 requirement for a high-altitude fighter equipped with a pressurised cabin. It was, therefore, fortunate, with the Welkin's fighting qualities falling short of expectations, that the expected attacks by the Luftwaffe's high-flying bombers did not materialise. The combination of these factors led to declining interest in, or indeed a requirement for, the aircraft as a high-altitude fighter. Nevertheless, seventy-seven were produced at Yeovil between 1940-45, though none ever served with an operational squadron. Whilst the Welkin could not claim any distinction in combat, it did play a pioneering role in the industry's upper-atmosphere research programme. Having entered the cabin air-conditioning business for the Welkin, Westland set up a special division to market the Westland Control Valve for what was fast becoming a standard high-altitude requirement in new-generation aircraft. Other companies, however, were reluctant to come to a potential competitor so Normalair Ltd was then founded as a separate subsidiary company in April 1946.

Harald Penrose prepares for the Welkin's first flight on 1 November 1942.

Less familiar shapes in Somerset's early wartime skies were the Curtiss Mohawk and Tomahawk fighters delivered to Westland for uncrating, assembly, and test after their sea voyage from the USA. This proved to be a time-consuming and, on occasion, costly and dangerous process, for it was found that the anti-corrosion fluid used to inhibit the engine cylinders and crankcase affected carburation and caused several engine failures in flight. Brought over as part of the Lend-Lease arrangement, the Mohawk was soon judged to be unsuited to the European combat environment, but the Tomahawk did gain a measure of success in the Middle East war theatre.

The Wyvern possessed the double distinction of being the first turboprop design to be produced by Westland, and the last fixed-wing propeller-driven fighter to be operated by the Royal Navy. The Rolls-Royce Eagle-powered prototype was the result of studies carried out in the latter stages of the Second World War, when interest was being shown in a long-range fighter for escort duties in the Far East. But again, as with the F.7/30 and the Whirlwind, it was the result of protracted engine development problems, not only with the Eagle, but those of its successor, the Clyde, that Wyvern deliveries were pushed ever backwards. It was only when, in May 1946, official instructions were given to investigate the replacement of the Clyde with the Armstrong Siddeley Python propeller-turbine that Westland's delivery programme began to move forward. Initial flight-testing did, however, begin with the Eagle, the most powerful and the last big piston-engine to be produced by Rolls-Royce. Six Eagle-powered Wyvern Mk1 prototypes carried out the initial flight test work, followed by later machines fitted with the Clyde and Python. It was, however, not until December 1952 that a final release for Service use was given for the Wyvern S. Mk4, No. 813 Squadron then giving up its Blackburn Firebrands to make way for the latest 'kid on the block'. A total of 124 Wyverns were built at Yeovil, which included thirty-seven prototypes and pre-production variants, and eighty-seven S. Mk4 production machines that finally equipped Royal Navy squadrons. As with several other notable fighter designs, the Wyvern, conceived during the war years, and powered by the ultimate in mechanically complex piston or turboprop powerplants, was overtaken in this transitional period by the much simpler turbojet-powered competition such as the Hawker Sea Hawk. As Harald Penrose so succinctly described it, the Wyvern was 'very nearly a good aircraft'.

The Welkin high-altitude fighter, though now fitted with Rolls-Royce Merlin engines, clearly reveals its Whirlwind ancestry.

Accidents will happen. This one occurred when the prototype Welkin experienced an engine failure when approaching Westland's airfield. Penrose managed to put the aircraft down in a field that later became the Yeovil showground off the Dorchester Road. This particular machine, DG558/G had the misfortune to suffer five forced landings within thirteen months!

Production Welkins await delivery to Service Maintenance Units, where many were soon reduced to scrap.

Westland fitted British radios and instruments to Curtiss Tomahawk (above) and Mohawk fighters which, though originally intended for French Air Force use, were diverted to the RAF under the Lease-Lend agreement. Harald Penrose regarded the Mohawk as the 'sweetest-handling' fighter he ever flew.

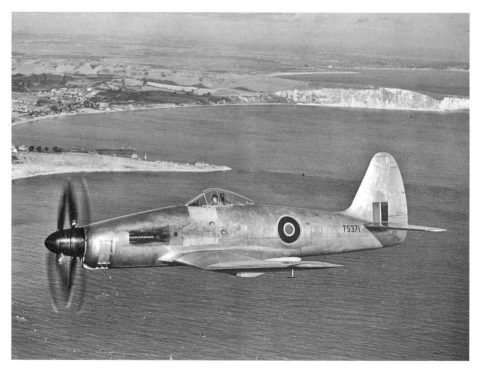

The Eagle-powered first prototype Wyvern shown flying off the South Coast on 15 October 1947. Moments later, following a propeller pitch change bearing failure, the aircraft crashed, killing Westland test pilot Peter Garner.

VP 109 was the first Wyvern TF. Mk 2 to be fitted with an Armstrong Siddeley Python engine. It was later partially converted to S. Mk 4 standard.

Wyvern S. Mk 4s of No. 813 Squadron, based at RNAS Ford, show the aggressive lines of Westland's last fighter design.

The Albacore and the accompanying Roc fighter never attained the fame of their more illustrious company stablemates, the Swordfish and the Skua. They did, however, form part of RNAS Yeovilton's air training establishment in the early days of the Second World War.

Chapter Six

Military Aviation in Somerset

Upon the outbreak of war, life in Somerset, as in most other counties, began to undergo a dramatic change. Prior to 1939, the main military air activity that had taken place involved Weston Zoyland, where, from the mid-1920s, target-towing Hawker Horsleys and, later, Hawker Henleys, provided anti-aircraft gunnery practice for locally based army units. The RAF also held summer camps at the Westland airfield in Yeovil, where, for example, Bristol F.2B Fighters and Armstrong Whitworth Siskins attended the event in 1930. In the late 1930s, radio-controlled DH Queen Bee targets were catapult-launched by No. 1 Anti-Aircraft Co-operation Unit at Watchet on the North Somerset coast. The standard of inter-Service gunnery did not, it may now be said, make dramatic calls on the public purse for replacement targets!

In 1940, the civil airports at Whitchurch and Weston-Super-Mare were immediately requisitioned by the Air Ministry, and work was also put into hand to provide military aerodromes at Yeovilton, Charmy Down, Charleton Horethorne, Lulsgate Bottom, Churchstanton, Merryfield, and Henstridge.

HMS *Heron*, a.k.a. RNAS Yeovilton, commissioned in June 1940, was, coincidentally, located on the Ilchester site originally selected in 1938 by Westland, then looking to expand its airfield capabilities. Even earlier, this inviting flat plain had come to the aid of an RAF pilot looking to land his Harrow bomber when faced with engine trouble.

Yeovilton's first training unit was No. 1 Naval Air Fighter School, where new pilots were taught air-combat tactics. Unfortunately, the lessons on offer were not absorbed quickly enough to deter the Luftwaffe mounting two minor raids on the station within a few weeks of its opening. The training of naval aircrew remained the station's primary role throughout the Second World War with, in the early period, aircraft such as the Sea Gladiator, Swordfish, Fulmar, Skua, and Roc the most prevalent types. As the war progressed, Defiants, Sea Hurricanes, Seafires, Martlets, Hellcats, Corsairs, and Barracudas arrived to provide more advanced training. The early ground-instructional aids may, with hindsight, be regarded as primitive and of some amusement. Not least of these were the specially adapted 'Stop Me and Buy One' Wall's Ice Cream tricycles used in 'D' School as 'bombers' and 'fighters', whilst under the control of trainee Air Direction Radar operators. Equipped with a compass, VHF receiver, headphones, and a metronome to control the pedalling rate, i.e., the 'aircraft's speed', the vehicles proved surprisingly effective in co-ordinating relative speeds and interception techniques. One famous trainee who experienced this 'high-tech' introduction was Kenneth More of 'Reach for the Sky' fame.

The Hawker Horsley performed in several roles for the RAF in the 1920s, including target-towing from Weston Zoyland.

Though originally intended as a dive-bomber, the Hawker Henley superseded the Horsley as the RAF's primary target tug.

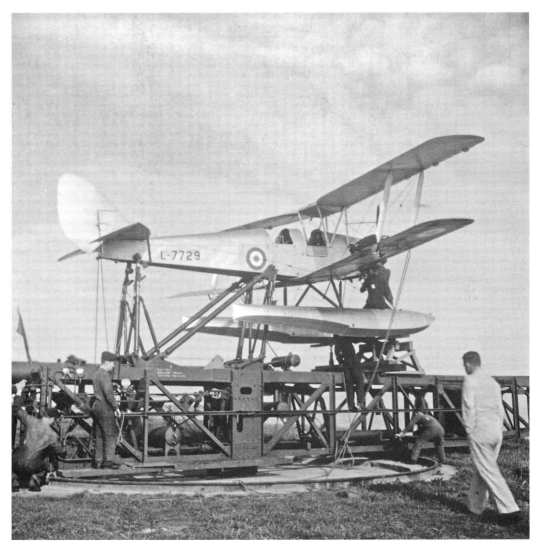

The radio-controlled DH Queen Bee was operated from Watchet on the North Somerset coast to provide pre-war gunnery practice for army and navy units.

Westland's airfield at Yeovil hosted RAF summer camps in the interwar period. Shown here are Armstrong Whitworth Siskins (above) and Bristol F.2b fighters on 8 September 1930.

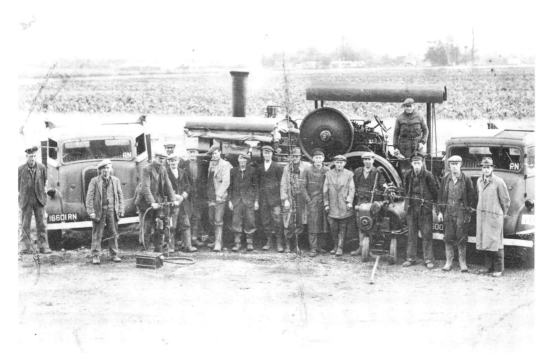

This could be the start of something big! The Yeovilton airfield construction crew in 1939.

It was an RAF Harrow that first touched down in what would later become RNAS Yeovilton – though through necessity rather than choice following an engine failure.

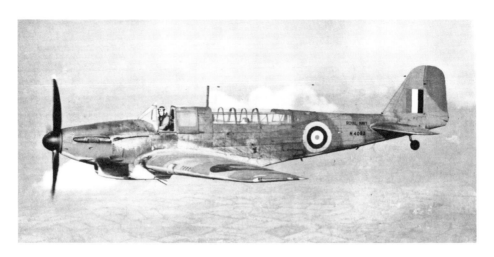

These pages: The Fleet Air Arm, though now no longer dependent on the RAF for its aircrew, was still in second place in the allocation of the best-quality machines. The Fulmar (top), Skua, and Roc, frequently in evidence at the navy's new base in its early days, were not on a par with the latest RAF counterparts. Ironically, the Swordfish, seemingly well outdated by the end of the 1930s, gained a war record that was second to none.

Yeovilton's role throughout the war was essentially linked to training. The busy skies saw more advanced types taking over with, for example, Martlets (top), Masters, and Fireflies now more capable of meeting the navy's requirements.

This is the first visit to RNAS Yeovilton of an American Corsair fighter in 1943. Note the Sea Gladiator, used for early morning 'met flights', vying for attention.

Actor Kenneth More relives his early ground-instruction days on the Wall's Ice Cream tricycle.

All part of the game! Ditching training for aircrew at Yeovil Baths.

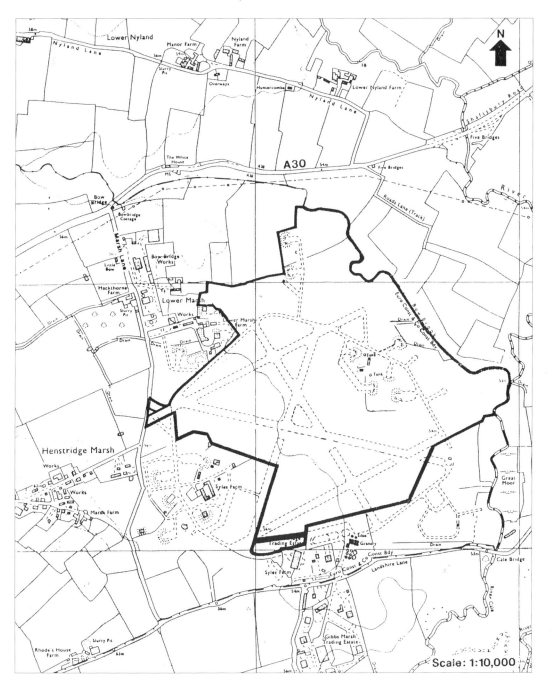

Henstridge was unusual in having a five-runway layout.

Seafires aplenty at Henstridge, as witnessed by these of No. 761 Squadron in 1943.

One of the reasons why the West Country featured so largely in training and working-up duties was that its greater distance from Luftwaffe bases reduced the possibility of inexperienced aircrew encountering enemy aircraft. Accordingly, with the demand for aircrew training increasing, a rudimentary station at Charleton Horethorne, originally intended as a secret satellite for the RAF at Exeter, was opened in May 1942 as HMS *Heron II*. It then undertook a variety of training roles in conjunction with its parent base at Yeovilton, but also, in March 1944, it was host to No. 765 Squadron's Travelling Research Unit, which, equipped with Wellingtons, moved around the country on 'recording duties' of a now somewhat indeterminate nature.

To the east of the county, RNAS Henstridge, now HMS *Dipper*, was commissioned in April 1943 as the primary base for type familiarisation and squadron work-up on Spitfires and Seafires.

Sited just three miles north of Bath, Charmy Down was opened in November 1940 as a satellite airfield for Colerne (Wiltshire). To bolster the air defence of Bristol and Bath, No. 87 Squadron moved in with its black-painted Hurricanes when the Luftwaffe's nocturnal raids began to increase. Night-fighting was not, however, the Hurricane's forte, nor indeed that of the Defiant, then being 'worked-up' by No. 125 Squadron, also based on this windy, exposed airfield. A more ambitious night-fighting approach saw the introduction of the twin-engined Douglas Havoc equipped with a nose-mounted

Just a few of the friends and foe who dropped in at Henstridge during the war years were a B-17 having lost a propeller (top), a Focke Wulf 190 serving as part of the Enemy Aircraft Evaluation flight, and a Curtiss Seamew, looking disproportionately tail heavy. The Seamew saw no operational service with the Royal Navy and was used solely for radio training by No. 755 Squadron at Worthy Down.

No. 736 Squadron's Fairey Barracudas, normally based at St Merryn in Cornwall, visiting Henstridge.

A chilly reminder of Henstridge in the bleak winter of 1944.

During the early part of the war, Charmy Down was home to the black-painted Hurricane (above) and Defiant night-fighters of Nos 87 and 125 Squadrons.

Although the introduction of the Douglas Havoc with a nose-mounted searchlight brought a more sophisticated approach to night interception, the success rate did not improve.

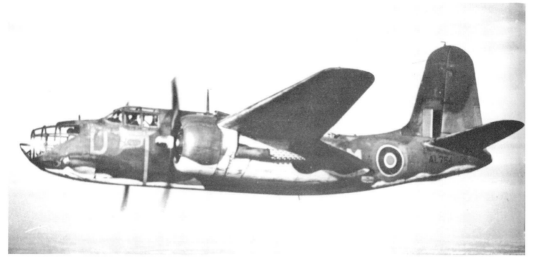

The Douglas Boston medium bomber saw extensive service with Allied air forces in the Second World War. RAF and Canadian squadrons operated from Charmy Down between 1941 and 1943.

Turbinlite searchlight. The idea was for the Havoc to track down a target using Airborne Interception radar, then illuminate it, thus allowing an accompanying Hurricane to carry out an attack. Successful interceptions, however, proved to be too difficult, and after a year, in January 1943, the Turbinlite aircraft at Charmy Down, and those at units elsewhere, were withdrawn from service. American-built Douglas Boston medium bombers were a common sight at this station between 1941 and 1943, with several Royal Canadian Air Force squadrons spending familiarisation periods alongside two operational squadrons, Nos 88 and 107, already equipped with the type.

By 1943, the Spitfire Mk Vb was being largely overtaken for front-line duties by later variants. Nevertheless, it was the mainstay of the Fighter Leaders' School when it opened in that year at Charmy Down.

Charmy Down's role changed again, when, in February 1943, the base became the home of the Fighter Leaders' School where thirty-six Spitfire Vs allowed flight and squadron commanders to put course theory into flying practice. Service movements were, of necessity, frequent during the war years, and so it proved, when, pending the arrival of USAAF personnel and aircraft, the station found itself temporarily housing 2,000 RAF Regiment officers and other ranks. Finally transferred to the IXth Air Force in February 1944, Charmy Down then became a Tactical Air Depot as preparations for D-Day got underway. By October, the airfield had reverted to RAF ownership, becoming a satellite for South Cerney (Gloucestershire), then part of 23 Group, Flying Training Command. Eventually decommissioned in 1946, the areas on either side of the A46, which saw so much training activity, have long since passed back into private ownership, leaving RAF Charmy Down now but a very distant memory.

These pages: Dangerous things, balloons! Especially when the mission entailed deliberately flying into the suspending cable, as the Research Flight crew of one Wellington based at Culmhead found out.

More towards the west, the airfield originally called Churchstanton, was opened in August 1941 as a typical three-runway fighter base and used exclusively by Nos 302 and 316 Squadrons of No. 2 Polish Fighter Wing. Though desperately keen to engage in aggressive combat, the Polish pilots had to settle for escorting bombers attacking the French ports and the occasional Channel fighter sweep until they were replaced by a Czech Wing in June 1942. It was excitement of a different, more controlled, type that attended the arrival that year of a special Research Flight from RAE Farnborough. This unit undertook the deliberate flying of Fairey Battles and Wellington bombers into barrage balloon cables to test the effectiveness of wing leading edge cutters. Such a task could only be described as 'downright dangerous', as proven when the Unit's CO, witnessing a balloon cable severing his aircraft's wing, called for an immediate evacuation of the aircraft!

In December 1943, the airfield was renamed Culmhead to avoid confusion with other bases now using the prefix 'Church'. A succession of squadron exchanges, all involving Spitfire variants, then led to armed reconnaissance and low-level strike operations over the D-Day period. Culmhead, however, saw itself briefly in the vanguard of aeronautical progress, when, just after the invasion, two Meteor jet fighters arrived for secret training. However, within a month, both aircraft had left for Manston in Kent, where new Meteor III squadrons were being formed to deal with the new German V-1 pilotless flying bomb, then menacing London and the Home Counties. What can only be described as minor training roles followed in the late and postwar periods, before, like so many companion airfields, Culmhead was officially closed in August 1946.

Though not in the first group of airfields to be constructed following the outbreak of war, work began in early 1943 to create a bomber station near Ilminster, some eight miles south-east of Taunton. Initially named Isle Abbots, it soon became a USAAF base, changing its name to Merryfield in the process. Between February 1944 and the invasion of Europe in June, the four squadrons of C-47s, comprising the 441st TCG, 50th TCW, IXth Troop Carrier Command, rehearsed their role for delivering the famed 82nd and 101st US Airborne Divisions to France.

Much curiosity was aroused at Culmhead, when, in mid-1944, two Meteor IIIs arrived for initial Service evaluation.

Merryfield was no stranger to the C-47s that delivered US airborne troops to France and returned the wounded to its 61st Field Hospital in 1944.

Tiger Moth trainers were everywhere, it seems, including the airfield at Weston-Super-Mare and its reserve landing ground at Lulsgate Bottom.

This Junkers 88A-4, 4D-DL of 3/KG30 landed in error at Broadfield Down (Lulsgate Bottom) after a night raid on Birkenhead.

Lysanders were a familiar sight when flying from Lulsgate Bottom on army co-operation work.

After D-Day, the 61st Field Hospital was established at Merryfield with 813 Air Evacuation Transport Squadron flying in a constant stream of casualties from the Normandy battlefield. By November, the Americans had departed, whereupon a succession of RAF Transport Command units were deployed, mainly on trooping duties to the Far East. Merryfield eventually ceased to be an operational station in October 1946.

The airfield at Lulsgate Bottom in North Somerset, was originally created in August 1940, as a Reserve Landing Ground for Tiger Moths operating from 10 Elementary Flying Training School at Weston-Super-Mare, but this relatively benign claim to fame was eclipsed when, at 06.20 on 24 July 1941, a Junkers 88A-4, 4D-DL of 3/KG30, its crew confused by RAF electronic countermeasures, landed on the ill-prepared runway. Within less than a year, however, its training function ceased, when it became a 10 Group fighter station. Whilst construction work was being carried out, the site was known as RAF Broadfield Down, but by January 1942, this had reverted to Lulsgate Bottom. Lysanders and Hurricanes belonging to No. 286 Squadron flew from here on army co-operation work until halfway through the year, when control of the station was passed, firstly, to 23 Group for Advanced Flying Unit pilot training and, later, to house a Flying Instructors School. In these various roles, Lulsgate Bottom served as a satellite for South Cerney (Glos), but following the disbandment of the school, it ended the war as a satellite for Upavon (Wilts). The station was placed on Care and Maintenance until 1947, when, after derequisitioning, the Ministry of Civil Aviation declared a bright new future for it as the new Bristol Airport.

IN COLLABORATION WITH

THE BRISTOL AEROPLANE CO., LTD.
GLOSTER AIRCRAFT CO., LTD. AND WESTLAND AIRCRAFT, LTD.

REQUEST THE PLEASURE OF YOUR COMPANY

ON THURSDAY, 30TH SEPTEMBER, 1948, AT 8.00 A.M.
AT THE NATIONAL CAR PARK, FRIDAY STREET, ST. PAUL'S CHURCHYARD, E.C.3

TO WITNESS THE DEPARTURE OF

THE BRISTOL HELICOPTER TYPE 171

ON THE INITIAL STAGE OF THE

FIRST CITY-CENTRE TO CITY-CENTRE FLIGHT
BETWEEN LONDON AND PARIS.

STAGES 2 AND 3 WILL BE COMPLETED BY THE

GLOSTER METEOR MK. VII AND THE WESTLAND-SIKORSKY S-51

COFFEE   INVITATION No. **311**

Although the formal amalgamation of helicopter companies in the 1950s had yet to take place, a distinct link had already taken place in 1948.

Chapter Seven

The Later Years

After the last Beaufighter had been delivered from Old Mixon in September 1945, the immediate postwar years saw the ex-shadow factories become engaged in the production of prefabricated houses to offset the severe destruction caused by air raids in Bristol. It was not until 1952 that aircraft work resumed at Old Mixon with the development and production of rocket motors, the refurbishment of Bristol gun turrets and the supply of assemblies for the Bristol Freighter and Britannia. In 1956, however, the pace stepped up when, due to pressure of work at Filton, Bristol transferred its helicopter design and production teams to what then became the Weston Division at Old Mixon. This move required the setting up of production lines for the Type 171 Sycamore, the Type 191 and 192 Belvedere tandem-rotor helicopters, and accommodating five Type 173 prototypes used for development test-flying. Work of this nature continued until 1960, when major changes within the industry, of which more later, brought the Bristol Company's helicopter activities under Westland control.

As already seen, the late 1940s saw the closure of many military airfields throughout the country. In Somerset, however, flying continued, for example, at Henstridge, where, in addition to naval flying training, the business adventurer Alan Bristow set up Air Whaling Ltd in 1953, with a mixed fleet of Dragonfly, Hiller 360, and Westland S 55 helicopters. Two years later, he formed Bristow Helicopters Ltd using four Westland Widgeons for oil exploration in the Persian Gulf. Today, although only one of its five original runways remains serviceable within what is now a large trading estate, Henstridge still provides a popular venue for vintage 'fly-in' events invariable organised by local light-aircraft enthusiast and aviation author Peter Campbell. It is also appropriate, considering how the counties' dividing line cuts across a corner of the airfield, that Henstridge is also home to the Dorset and Somerset Air Ambulance Service which, since 2007, has operated a Eurocopter EC 135.

Elsewhere in the county, at Weston Zoyland, a variety of postwar training programmes involved glider trials using Vultee Vengeance tugs and, when the Korean War gathered pace, the opening, in 1952, of 209 Advanced Flying School (later renamed 12 Flying Training School), equipped with Vampires and Meteors. An unusual departure was the forming of an air element for the British Atomic Task Force in November 1955. This comprised a number of Canberra B6s and PR7s, along with three Varsity trainers, which were later to assist in atomic bomb trials in Australia.

The Bristol Sycamore assembly line at Old Mixon in the late 1950s.

First flight of XG 447, the prototype Type 192 at the Weston Division airfield on 5 July 1958.

A truly beautiful study. The prototype Belvedere obligingly poses over the Beach Lawns at Weston-Super-Mare. The airfield at Old Mixon is in the far distance.

Naval training continued at Henstridge until the station closed in 1957. Here, an RNVR pilot undergoes bale-out practice from a Seafire XVII.

Hawker Sea Fury FB.11s were regular visitors to Henstridge.

The S-51 Dragonfly, Westland's first postwar rotary-wing venture, formed part of the Bristow Air Whaling helicopter fleet at Henstridge.

Bristow Helicopters Ltd employed four Widgeons for oil exploration in the Middle East. This picture shows a Widgeon at Yeovil with an Eagle-powered Wyvern in the background.

Though once owned and stored for several years at Henstridge by businessman Brian Woodford, this superbly finished DH.89 Rapide, G-ACZE, now resides with Chewton Glen Aviation on the Isle of Wight.

This attractive visitor to a Henstridge 'fly-in' is a DH.60X Moth, which, though not carrying a British civil registration, displays an American identifier, N565M on the rudder.

Visiting Henstridge sometime before it was destroyed in the arson attack at Old Sarum in January 1987 is the Lockspeiser LDA-01, G-AVOR. A larger version of this utility aircraft, though planned, was never built.

The Vultee Vengeance was an import from America under the Lend-Lease scheme. A small number were used by No. 587 Squadron at Weston Zoyland for target-towing.

Meteor T.7s being refuelled for a training sortie at Weston Zoyland's 209 AFS.

The Vampire FB.5 also formed part of Flying Training Command's activities at Weston Zoyland.

Above: No. 542 Squadron equipped with Canberra B6s was the last RAF unit to operate from Weston Zoyland before it closed in 1957.

Opposite: Merryfield, showing its standard three-runway layout in 1964. Westland carried out test-flying alongside RAF and Royal Navy units throughout the 1950s.

Merryfield was used throughout the 1950s by Westland for flight-testing Wyverns and also Meteors and Sabres that had been refurbished at the company's Ilchester repair unit. One particularly interesting development contract undertaken by Westland at the airfield was the modification of a Meteor F.4 (RA 490), fitted with specially adapted Nene engines, for deflected jet trials. Although flight tests indicated a large reduction of 40 kts in stalling speed, the feature was not carried over into production. Service flying was resumed when the station was re-activated by Flying Training Command in 1951, Vampire FB 5s and Meteor T7s dominating the scene until 1955. Following its transfer to 1 Group Bomber Command, the photo-reconnaissance Canberras of 231 Operational Conversion Unit moved in but remained in residence only until the end of 1956. The RAF's departure neatly coincided with the navy's need to temporarily house the Sea Venoms of No. 766 and other operational squadrons whilst RNAS Yeovilton underwent extensive reconstruction.

After reverting to Care and Maintenance in 1958, this once-busy site became derelict, but it was granted another lease of life when, in 1972, it was restored as a satellite for Yeovilton, becoming HMS *Heron*, RNAS Merryfield. Since then, although the runways are no longer serviceable, it has provided training facilities for Commando helicopter squadrons and remains a haven for flying model aircraft devotees.

Westland installed Nene engines in this Meteor F.4 (RA490) for jet deflector trials, at Merryfield.

Wyverns and Sabres, shown here, were overhauled at Westland's Ilchester facility and test-flown at Merryfield.

Most notably, Yeovilton, presently home to Nos 815 and 702 (Lynx) alongside 846 and 845 (Sea King) Squadrons, also accommodates the Royal Navy's Historic Flight, the Fleet Requirements and Air Direction Unit (FRADU) and the Fleet Air Arm Museum. Large crowds are guaranteed to attend the West Country's biggest air display, which has been an annual feature at the base since 1945.

Unsurprisingly, Yeovilton has seen or been home to every type of fixed and rotary-wing machine to serve with the Royal Navy in the postwar period. Examples of these are shown in the following pages.

Yeovilton's Air Day has proved a major 'crowd-puller' since the first held in 1945. Shown here, left to right, are a Sea Fury, Firefly, Swordfish, and a Blackburn Firebrand.

The Firefly, Sea Fury, and Fairey Swordfish of the Royal Navy's Historic Flight, which was founded in 1972.

Yeovilton's Swordfish appeared as LS 423 in the film *Sink the Bismarck*.

Shown here is Sea Vixen XJ 576 of No. 899 Squadron, loading 2-inch rockets in 1962.

The Buccaneer S. Mk 1s of No. 801 Squadron. Lt Cdr Ted Anson briefs his crews at Yeovilton on 12 March 1963.

No. 700L Squadron was a joint Royal Navy/Royal Netherlands Navy Intensive Flying Trials Unit formed in September 1976 to evaluate the Lynx.

The Sea King demonstrates its lifting capability over a miscellany of Hunters, Sea Harriers and F 104 Starfighters in 1980.

Although BAe Hawks have now replaced the Hunters shown here and the Canberra is no longer in service, the Fleet Requirements and Air Direction Unit (FRADU) is still based at Yeovilton. It works in conjunction with Cobham Aviation Services' Falcon 20 aircraft to provide electronic warfare training.

Of no small significance was the decision, taken in 1947, to transfer the site and title of Bristol Airport from Whitchurch, then rapidly being overtaken by the encroachment of local building work, to Lulsgate Bottom. This choice was the final outcome of much heated local debate, for the Filton airfield had also proved to be an attractive contender. However, the demands of the Bristol Aeroplane Company for test-flying conflicted strongly with those of a developing airport and the option was not pursued. It was not until after Bristol Corporation's purchase of the 300-acre Lulsgate site in 1955 that major 'earth turning' began, but since then, major ongoing improvements have seen the 'new' location, with its extended runways, state-of-the-art landing aids and terminal facilities, consolidate its place as the West Country's main point of air embarkation. A measure of its subsequent expansion may be gained from the increase in annual passenger transportation from some 33,000 in 1957 – the year of the airport's formal opening – to what is now a projected target of 10 million for 2019/20. Today, in 2010, the airport is a thriving hub serving the needs of fourteen airlines and some sixty tour operators, with Continental Airlines currently providing the most far-reaching link to Newark, New Jersey, in the USA.

Lulsgate Aerodrome, *c.* 1946.

The Duchess of Kent opens the new Bristol Airport at Lulsgate in May 1957.

This Bristol Britannia in British Overseas Airways Corporation livery evokes strong memories of Lulsgate in the late 1950s

An Aviation Trader's Carvair provides 'garaging space' for a BMC Farina design, probably a Morris Oxford or a Austin Cambridge, at Lulsgate in 1967.

A Channel Airways Hawker Siddeley Trident, a Britannia Airways Boeing 737 and an Autair BAC1-11 aircraft. The DC3 belonged to Dan Air.

The Fairey Aviation Company in Hayes possessed excellent design teams that, in the postwar period, produced the Gannet, the FD.1 and FD.2 supersonic research aircraft and a series of rotary-winged machines that culminated in the highly advanced Rotodyne, shown here.

Chapter Eight

Somerset – The Helicopter County

At the end of the Wyvern fighter programme in the early 1950s, Westland diverted its main energies into the rotary-winged aircraft market. This change of direction had already begun when, in January 1947, an initial licence agreement was reached with America's United Aircraft Corporation to produce the Sikorsky S-51, though using British materials and incorporating a British Alvis Leonides engine. This proved to be a highly significant breakthrough for the company, with orders quickly following for both Service and civil variants of what then became the Dragonfly. A total of 149 were eventually built, which, soon followed by the larger S-55 Whirlwind, made severe demands on Westland's manufacturing capabilities. However, the company later found itself faced with far bigger challenges. Changes imposed by the government in the early 1960s decreed that the rotary-wing projects then being undertaken by the Bristol, Saunders-Roe, and Fairey companies were now to be absorbed into a new wholly owned company, Westland Helicopters Ltd. This rationalisation, which placed the future of the British helicopter industry firmly in Westland's hands was clearly influenced by the range of skills and experience in rotary-wing aircraft manufacture already evident at Yeovil and at nearby Old Mixon, where the assembly, repair, and in-service support of helicopters would continue until the factory's closure in September 2002. This proved to be a turbulent period for the entire industry, for the helicopter companies' amalgamation had to be carried out in parallel with the consolidation of virtually all of the fixed-wing aircraft companies into two major groups, the British Aircraft Corporation and the Hawker Siddeley Group (soon to be renamed Hawker Siddeley Aviation Ltd). In addition to all this, Westland became the major shareholder in yet another new concern, the British Hovercraft Company, which, formed out of Saunders-Roe, was to consolidate the development of this revolutionary type of craft. Understandably, these political directives caused great dismay within the affected companies with many employees either unable or unwilling to relocate homes and families. However, this restructuring, forced into being by intense global competition and though painful at times, did bring together at Yeovil a concentration of expertise and experience that proved the basis of today's highly motivated design and production teams.

The British aerospace industry has, since its founding, enjoyed many successes and suffered many setbacks. That which attended the cancellation of the Fairey Rotodyne in February 1962, it having by then come under the Westland umbrella, was a particularly bitter pill to swallow. This large, turbo-propeller-driven compound helicopter represented a major leap forward in design, employing fuel-burning pressure-jet units on each

Whirlwind assembly at Yeovil in the early 1950s. Note the two Wyverns in the top right-hand corner.

rotor-blade tip. Though initially capturing worldwide civil and military interest, it was later considered to be excessively noisy for intercity use, and despite Fairey's claim that noise-reduction schemes were well in hand, the government's refusal to provide further development funding finally brought about its demise. This proved to be a double blow for Yeovil, as Westland's own large heavy-lift helicopter, the Westminster, had been abandoned two years previously when it was thought that the Rotodyne, being a more advanced concept, would capture the market. Despite these early disappointments, Westland Helicopters proved its flexibility when, within the Anglo-French Helicopter Package Deal finally agreed in 1967, it combined with Aérospatiale to produce the French Puma and Gazelle and the British WG-13, which later became the Lynx. After appearing in many variant forms since its first flight in March 1971, the Lynx is still attracting orders today, with the total built now approaching 500. Worthy of mention at this point is the achievement of a Westland Lynx, G-LYNX, flown by chief test pilot Trevor Eggington with Derek Clews as flight-test engineer on 11 August 1986, when, racing across the Somerset Levels at 400.87 kph (249.10 mph), it set up world helicopter records for Absolute Speed and for helicopters in the 3,000-4,500kg weight band, records which, at the time of writing in 2010, are still unbeaten!

As part of the absorption of Fairey in 1960 Westland took on the overhaul, refurbishment, and modernisation programmes for the Gannet. These were initially carried out at Ilchester, with flying from Yeovilton, before the work was transferred to Old Mixon, shown here, in 1970. The last Gannet AEW Mk 3, XL 494, to leave Old Mixon in February 1976 is shown below.

Westland built two Westminster heavy-lift helicopters, which attracted the description of 'flying cut-away drawings'! Their development did not survive the amalgamation of the other helicopter manufactures, particularly that of Fairey with the Rotodyne.

The Westland Wessex entered and remained in production from the early 1960s. It was the world's first quantity-produced helicopter to incorporate a free gas turbine. Here, Dr Hislop hands over XV732 to the CO of the Queen's Flight in 1969.

Westland Wessex XV 732 undergoing acceptance flying over local landmark, Berrow Mump.

Gazelle production in full flow at Yeovil.

AgustaWestland's erstwhile Chief Flight Test Engineer and present archivist David Gibbings vividly recalls the Lynx record breaking flight in this highly evocative painting.

Undoubtedly one of the most controversial political decisions that affected the aerospace industry and which led to the resignation of Defence Secretary Michael Heseltine, and Leon Brittan, then the Industry Secretary, was that brought about by the so-called 'Westland Affair' in 1986-87. The issue was relatively simple, but the political ramifications were complex and deeply divisive. With Westland then desperately in need of extra funds to survive, did the US or the European offer of collaboration provide the best line of financial rescue? This highly charged situation was finally resolved when the American United Technologies group became a major shareholder in Westland, albeit bringing with it an agreeable inducement that allowed the Sikorsky Black Hawk to be built under licence as the WS-70 at Yeovil. Whilst at that time the American offer was considered by the Westland board and Mrs Thatcher's main Cabinet to be the preferred option, the outbreak of the Gulf War later brought political and commercial differences that resulted in Sikorsky withdrawing its holdings and rescinding the licence to build the Black Hawk.

European alliance surfaced again, however, when, in the 1980s, Westland and Agusta, having earlier worked together to produce the Sioux light helicopter, found themselves

The first and third prototype EH 101s over familiar Somerset countryside in 1988.

again teamed up, this time as European Helicopter Industries, to develop and produce the EH 101. This followed the signing of a Memorandum of Agreement between the British and Italian governments in 1979. This was a time when large technical developments were taking place in materials, avionics and rotor design, all of which contributed to a difficult sharing of the work and an extended flight-test programme. By 1990, with most of the technical issues resolved, the major outstanding question lay with which company was to be Prime Contractor for the Royal Navy's aircraft. The difficulty here was that the Prime Contractor had to be able to underwrite any shortfall in contractual compliance and not even the combined resources of the two companies could meet this requirement. The problem was eventually overcome when the first production order for 44 Merlin HM Mk1s was placed with Lockheed-Martin, but when, in 1994, Westland became part of the Guest, Keen & Nettlefold (GKN) group and able to call upon greater financial resources, it successfully re-bid to become Prime Contractor.

As the decade progressed, GKN-Westland, with the Merlin now well underway, won the contract to supply the Anglicised version of the Boeing (McDonnell-Douglas)

Whilst a civil version of the EH 101 appeared as the Heliliner in 1990, the first Royal Navy acceptance trials of the Service variant, the Merlin, began a year later.

The UK Apache's first flight over the Westland factory on 26 August 1999. Sixty-seven were ordered for the British Army Air Corps.

Apache attack helicopter to the British Army. The merging of Westland into the GKN group broadly coincided with that of Agusta into Finmeccanica, whereupon, in 2001, both parent organisations saw the synergy to be gained by combining their helicopter assets under one name – AgustaWestland. But the story doesn't, by any means, end there, because in 2005, GKN sold its holdings, leaving Westland as a direct and essential part of the Italian company. Today, Westland is one of the last of the original names associated with the birth of aircraft manufacture in Britain, yet it proudly survives in a world aerospace market, every aspect of which is completely multinational and disregarding of geographical location. Would such affiliations, one may wonder, have been uppermost in John Stringfellow's mind over a century and a half ago? Unlikely indeed, for the county's pioneer was all too occupied with simply getting an adequately powered flying machine into the air. Twentieth and twenty-first century problems with the mechanics and political problems of flight would have had to take their place in a very long queue!

In considering Somerset's claim to be the 'helicopter county', and seemingly the exclusive province of AgustaWestland, one must pause and also give thought to the essential role played by the Royal Navy's 'whirlybirds' at Yeovilton. The introduction of the Dragonfly into service saw the helicopter soon overtake the destroyer as 'rescue

Westland Whirlwinds on board HMS *Bulwark* in 1957. This type had performed the first vertical assault, at Suez, a year earlier.

ship' when following aircraft carriers during 'flying stations'. This proved to be the first step in the gradual transition of the Fleet Air Arm to becoming an entirely rotary-wing service.

Following on from the Dragonfly, the arrival of the Sikorsky S-55 Whirlwind gave the British Services a completely new outlook on the use of the helicopter, not only with regard to Search and Rescue operations but, with the advent of 'dipping sonar' its growing importance in anti-submarine warfare. The Whirlwind remained in service until well into the 1970s, with a final total of 364 leaving the Yeovil production line. By that time, naval policy no longer embraced the need for fixed-wing anti-submarine aircraft, nor, indeed, the requirement for large aircraft carriers, though it would appear that, subject to political vicissitudes, these are scheduled to reappear in the foreseeable future!

At Yeovilton, despite the inevitable departure of the navy's front-line jet squadrons, fixed-wing operations remained very much in evidence with the Fleet Requirements Unit's Hunters and, later, Hawks working alongside civilian contractors Airwork Ltd and FR Aviation Ltd to provide sea-to-air electronic-warfare defence training for NATO-country navies. This facility continues today with Cobham Aviation Services UK fleet of Dassault Falcon 20s working in tandem with Yeovilton's Fleet Requirements and

Hunter T.8s of the Royal Navy's Fleet Requirements Unit on parade at Yeovilton.

Cobham Aviation Services' Falcon 20s (note the underwing electronic-threat simulation pods) now operate in tandem with navy FRADU Hawks for defence training.

Development Unit (FRADU) aircraft to provide sea-skimming missile-threat simulation training.

Yeovilton's primary role has, in recent times, been to accommodate the Commando Helicopter Units. Nos 707 and 846 Squadrons, equipped with the Westland Wessex HU 5 aircraft, were the first to arrive in May 1972.

The Lynx first made its presence felt when, in 1976, No. 700L Squadron was formed in conjunction with the Royal Netherlands Navy. Just two years later, the withdrawal of the navy's Phantoms, Buccaneers, and Gannets saw the Westland Sea King begin to eclipse the Wessex in Commando service. Thereafter, not only was the Sea King a constant presence in Yeovilton's skies but the Sea Harriers of No. 700A Squadron Intensive Flying Trials Unit now resident on the base, also added a few decibels to the noisy chorus!

Even though, in the Second World War, Yeovilton was not called upon to act as a front-line station, later changes in the naval command structure meant that, by the time of the Falklands War in 1982, it was required to supply trained units for immediate operational duty. Accordingly, Nos 800 and 801 Squadrons (Sea Harrier) and Nos 845 and 846 Squadrons (Sea King) were deployed to the southern war theatre. For a more definitive description of the part played by Yeovilton's RN aircraft and personnel over the years, see 'Yeovilton' in Recommended Reading.

Yeovilton, the kingdom of Wessex! Wessex HU 5s of Nos 707, 845, and 856 Naval Air Squadrons prepare to take part in the Fleet Review off Spithead on 28 June 1977. This was to celebrate the Queen's Silver Jubilee.

Time to say farewell! Symbolic of the withdrawal of the navy's fixed-wing aircraft, Phantom XT 596 lands at Yeovilton after its very last flight. It now forms an impressive exhibit in the Fleet Air Arm Museum.

No. 707 Squadron Sea King HC 4s present their 'party piece' over Yeovilton's Sea Harriers and Canberras in December 1985.

The Sea Harrier became battle-hardened in a hurry during the Falklands War in 1982. Here, XZ 496 of No. 800 Squadron returns to HMS *Hermes* after a Combat Air Patrol.

It is hoped that from these necessarily abbreviated chapters, Somerset can be seen to have contributed greatly to British aviation. With the AgustaWestland AW159 Lynx Wildcat now undergoing flight-testing and due to become operational with the British Army in 2014 and the Royal Navy in 2015, Somerset's claim to be 'Helicopter County' is, it seems, unlikely to be challenged for many years to come.

Home from the Falklands! Sea Harriers and Sea Kings line the deck of HMS *Hermes* as she nears Portsmouth.

Recommended Reading

Somerset At War, Mac Hawkins (The Dovecote Press).
Somewhere in the West Country, Ken Wakefield (Crecy Publishing).
Westland Aircraft since 1915, Derek James (Putnam Aeronautical Books)
Westland, Derek James (Tempus Publishing)
Yeovilton, Cdr P. M. Rippon & Graham Mottram (Fox & Co.).
Action Stations: 5. Military Airfields of the South-West, Chris Ashworth (Patrick Stephens).
Fairey Rotodyne, David Gibbings (The History Press)
The Forgotten Pilots, Lettice Curtis (Westward Digital Ltd)

Also Available from Amberley Publishing

Home Guard Manual 1941

£7.99
ISBN: 978 1 4456 0047 5

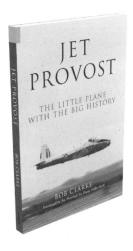

Jet Provost
The Little Plane with the Big History
Bob Clarke

£19.99
ISBN: 978 1 84868 097 5

We're Here to Win the War for You
The US 8th Airforce at War
Martin W. Bowman

£18.99
ISBN: 978 1 84868 429 4